W9-DEC-050

Japanese Culture

Teresa Heapy

Heinemann
LIBRARY

Chicago, Illinois

www.capstonepub.com
Visit our website to find out more information about Heinemann-Raintree books.

To order:
☎ Phone 800-747-4992
🖳 Visit www.capstonepub.com to browse our catalog and order online.

Edited by Charlotte Guillain, Abby Colich, and Vaarunika Dharmapala
Designed by Steve Mead
Original illustrations © Capstone Global Library Ltd 2013
Illustrations by Oxford Designers & Illustrators
Picture research by Ruth Blair

Originated by Capstone Global Library Ltd
Printed in the United States of America in North Mankato, Minnesota.
062013   007580RP

16 15 14 13
10 9 8 7 6 5 4 3

Library of Congress Cataloging-in-Publication Data
Heapy, Teresa.
  Japanese culture / Teresa Heapy.—1st ed.
     p. cm.—(Global cultures)
  Includes bibliographical references and index.
  ISBN 978-1-4329-6780-2 (hb)—ISBN 978-1-4329-6789-5 (pb) 1. Culture—History. 2. Japan—Social life and customs. 3. Japan—Civilization. I. Title.
  HM621.H423 2013

Acknowledgments
We would like to thank the following for permission to reproduce photographs: Corbis pp. 6 (© Mike Watson/moodboard), 7 (© Christine Schneider), 10 (© Paulo Fridman), 12 (© Issei Kato/Reuters), 15 (© Bloomimage), 21 (© WWD/Condé Nast), 24 (© Frank Robichon/EPA), 31 (© Michael S. Yamashita), 33 (© Charles Platiau/Reuters), 36 (© Ton Koene/ZUMA Press), 40 (© Michael S. Yamashita); Photolibrary pp. 18, 22, 27, 30, 36, 37, 38, 41; Photolibrary p. 28 (Image Source); © Photoshot pp. 19 (TIPS), 25; Photoshot pp. 8 (© Mixa), 20 (© Imagebrokers), 35 (© Royalty-Free/Corbis), 39 (© Bloomberg News/Landov); Shutterstock p. 5 (© Jules_Kitano), 13 (© akiyoko), 16 (© Mariya Dimova), 17 (© Tristan Scholze), 18 (© Thomas La Mela), 23 (© MNStudio), 26 (© Angela N. Hunt), 34 (© Timmary), 43 top left (© Huang Yuetao), 43 top right (© Paskee), 43 bottom left (© Paolo Gianti), 43 bottom right (© Yury Zap), design features (© Pavol Kmeto).

Cover photograph of a smiling Japanese girl reproduced with permission of Alamy (© Travel Pictures). Cover design feature of a colorful parasol reproduced with permission of Shutterstock (© Pavol Kmeto).

CONTENTS

Some words are shown in bold, **like this**. You can find out what they mean by looking in the glossary.

INTRODUCING JAPANESE CULTURE

What do you picture when you think of Japanese **culture**? Do you think of gardens full of cherry blossom trees or of **manga** cartoons? Do you picture high-rise buildings or ancient **temples**?

Japan is in East Asia, and is made up of a long string of islands. It stretches for around 1,500 miles (2,414 kilometers). It has four main islands: Hokkaido, Shikoku, Kyushu, and Honshu, where you will find the capital city, Tokyo. Japan also has about 4,000 other islands!

What is culture?

Culture includes the values, beliefs, and attitudes of a particular place. It is about how people live and worship and about the music, art, and literature they produce. Japan is an astonishing, exciting country with a unique culture that embraces both Western influences and Eastern traditions. It is also one of the world's most economically and technologically advanced societies.

Japan has theater, art, games, and **ceremonies** that go back centuries. It is also at the cutting edge of new computer technologies. The simple beauties of nature are very valued, but Japan is also famous for its intricate designs on fabrics and pottery. There are traditional ceremonies and customs that can seem formal and controlled, but the Japanese people also have a lot of fun!

Japan has many amazing temples, which are set in beautiful gardens.

FAMILY AND SOCIETY

Family plays a strong part in Japanese lives. Most families live together within a **nuclear family**, with a mother, father, and children. Grandparents often live hundreds of miles away.

In previous generations, it was considered ideal for a family to live together with grandparents in an "extended" family. After World War II (1939–1945), when Japan's industries were expanding and people had to live near their place of work, this was no longer possible for everyone. However, on national holidays, families often travel to visit grandparents.

Japanese fathers usually work long hours, while mothers are often full-time homemakers. In recent years, more women have started to work outside the home, but generally only when they have someone to care for their children.

A sense of loyalty and respect toward one's family is very important in Japanese culture.

Hierarchies and customs

The Japanese have a great sense of **hierarchy**, duty, and loyalty. This can be the case in their family or in an organization—for example, in their workplace or at school.

Japanese life is based on a series of groups: family, social, school, and business. People tend to address each other by the names of their positions—for example, *sensei* (teacher). The Japanese language requires most polite conversation to include a level of respect.

On means the debt or obligation that people have to all others, particularly those who have shown them kindness. The biggest debt for the Japanese is to their parents.

Did you know?

Bowing (*ojigi*) is important in Japan: people bow to each other rather than shaking hands. Bowing is a gesture of respect, and it can mean many things, from "I'm sorry" to "congratulations."

Houses

Traditional Japanese homes looked very different from Western houses. They had sliding doors to divide the living space and *tatami* mats (made from woven grass) on the floor. Japanese people used to sit directly on the *tatami*, or on cushions called *zabuton*. This is why people always take off their shoes when entering a Japanese house.

Modern Japanese houses often look like Western homes on the inside. If they have room, some people may keep one traditionally styled room (*washitsu*) with *tatami* matting and sliding doors. There are many high-rise buildings in the major cities, and about one-quarter of Japanese people live in Tokyo.

This is what a traditional Japanese room might look like. You can see the *tatami* mats and the *zabuton* cushions on the floor.

School

The school year in Japan starts in April. Children start school at three years old and go to kindergarten. They start elementary school when they are six and attend this for six years, until they are twelve. They then go to middle or junior high school until they are 15, when they have to take an entrance exam in order to get into senior high school.

Children often attend lots of clubs after school, including music, sports, and science clubs. They sometimes go to *juku* (private "cram" schools) that help them to perform at their best and ensure they get into the best senior high schools.

Students study subjects such as mathematics and science, but they also study **calligraphy** (*shodo*) and **haiku**. A haiku is a short poem that is made up of exactly 17 **syllables**.

Shodo involves writing Japanese characters in an artistic style. Normally, Japanese people use pens or pencils to write. In *shodo*, they write with a special paintbrush dipped into ink. At the beginning of each year, children take part in *kakizome*, in which they create a piece of calligraphy to express their wishes for the new year.

YOUNG PEOPLE

Earthquakes are common in Japan. The 2011 earthquake and tsunami devastated the country and killed over 22,000 people. Japanese schools hold monthly earthquake drills. Children learn to get under their desks, head first, and hold onto the legs of the desk until the earthquake is over.

CEREMONY
AND BELIEFS

Japan is famous for its many varied and beautiful celebrations. It has lots of traditions and customs that date from ancient times, with some coming directly from the Shinto and **Buddhist** religions.

This is the Heian Jingu, a Shinto shrine in Kyoto.

Shinto

Shinto is the oldest Japanese religion. Followers of Shintoism worship gods and goddesses called *kami*. *Kami* are thought to be the essential divine forces in living beings and nature, including rivers, mountains, and trees. Followers also believe *kami* are present in creativity, growth, and healing.

There are thousands of Shinto **shrines** in Japan. Some can even be found at the sides of roads. The shrines often use nature in some way or use symbols of nature, such as water, trees, or stones.

Buddhism

Many Japanese families have a particular connection to a Buddhist temple where funeral and memorial services for members of their family are performed. Buddhists believe in a continuing cycle of death and rebirth, with each person's position and well-being in one life being determined by his or her behavior in a previous life. **Meditation**, in many forms, is central to Buddhism.

Did you know?

One of the best-known types of meditation is Zen. Zen meditation involves clearing the mind and controlling the breathing, in order to create a calm state of mind. It gives people a chance to think about themselves in a **spiritual** way and allows them to step outside everyday life.

Festivals

Japan has 15 national holidays. New Year's Day (*Oshogatsu*) is traditionally seen as the most important. People send *nengajo*, or New Year's cards, to arrive on New Year's Day.

During New Year's Day celebrations, bells are rung 108 times in Buddhist temples across Japan, to symbolize the 108 sins in Buddhist belief.

Every year, at midnight on December 31, millions of people visit Shinto shrines and Buddhist temples to pray for the safety, happiness, and long lives of their families. Celebrations continue for three days after this, with people visiting family and friends. They eat special food, called *osechi-ryori*, which is beautiful to look at. *Osechi-ryori* is made of ingredients that will keep for several days, to help avoid the need for cooking and shopping during the celebrations.

Celebrating children

Japan has special celebration days for children. The *Shichi-go-san* ("seven-five-three") festival falls on November 15 and celebrates children who are reaching the ages of seven, five, and three. These ages are considered to be important by the Japanese, as odd numbers are thought to be lucky. The family visits a shrine together and gives the child some *chitose-ame* (a "thousand years" candy), which is presented in a special bag.

Children's Day is celebrated in Japan on May 5 each year. Events involving children are held all over the country. Families with young boys fly *koinobori* (carp kites) in front of their houses. Carp are fish and are a symbol of success, determination, and a long life. This stems from a Chinese legend about a brave carp that became a dragon.

Did you know?

This is how to say "Happy New Year" in Japanese: *Akemashite omedeto gozaimasu!*

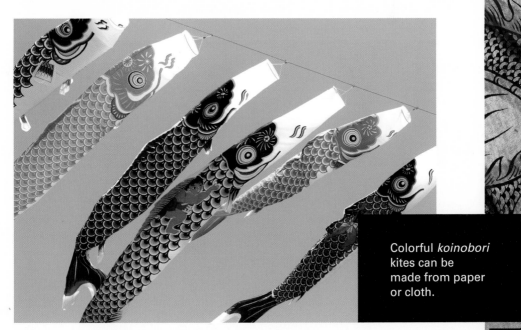

Colorful *koinobori* kites can be made from paper or cloth.

Tea ceremonies

A tea ceremony (*chado*) is based on an ancient tradition that brings together four ideas: harmony with people and nature, respect for others, purity of heart and mind, and tranquillity (peace). *Chado* grew from the custom of Zen Buddhist monks drinking tea together from a single bronze bowl.

Each step of the preparation has very particular movements, and the equipment is very carefully chosen and placed. It is all done very carefully by the host, who could be an expert tea-master but could also be an ordinary person. It is an opportunity to forget about time and the everyday world.

Tea ceremonies take place in a tea-house (*cha-shitsu*), which can be a room in a house, a small building away from the house, or in a shrine.

Preparing for tea ceremonies takes a lot of time, money, and thought. There are many different types of tea equipment— for example, the *chashaku* is a bamboo spoon for scooping up tea. Some of the equipment can be very expensive. The ceremonies are performed at particular times of year— for example, on New Year's Day.

Did you know?

The study of the tea ceremony can take many years to learn. The tea-master must be familiar with the production and types of tea, the **kimono** (the robe worn by the host), calligraphy, the incense burned to create a calming aroma, the china cups and pots used, and other traditions.

A tea ceremony
can last between
one and five hours.

15

Cherry blossom ceremonies

Japan is famous for its cherry blossoms (*sakura*) in spring. The blossoms on cherry trees mean much more to the Japanese than just spring flowers. They represent the end of winter and the beginning of new spring life. The cherry blossom is a well-known symbol of Japan and is frequently shown on traditional Japanese goods and art.

Cherry blossoms usually appear from late March to early May. The period between late April and early May is known as Golden Week. Golden Week is a time when many people take vacations, since there are so many public holidays and celebrations, including May Day and Children's Day.

Cherry blossoms appear on the trees before the leaves appear.

Large crowds of people gather for *hanami* celebrations wherever cherry blossom trees can be found.

Hanami

Hanami (flower viewing) is the traditional Japanese custom of enjoying the cherry blossoms. The tradition is many centuries old and is said to have started during the Nara period (710–784 CE). *Hanami* celebrations involve huge outdoor parties beneath the cherry blossoms, during the day or night. Outdoor lanterns are hung on the trees when the celebrations occur at night. These parties can be with family, friends, or coworkers. They are held in parks, temple or shrine grounds, or streets lined with trees.

Did you know?

During spring, there are nightly television blossom forecasts announced by the weather center. Everyone watches very carefully, as the blossoms only last a week or two!

ORNAMENT

Traditional Japanese artistic taste combines delicacy with simplicity, as seen, for example, in woodcarvings, calligraphy, and paintings. Modern Japanese artistic forms, such as manga and **anime** (pronounced AN-ih-may), are bolder, but also very simple and dramatic. They are very popular all over the world.

Did you know?

The name *Kenrokuen* means "six attributes (features)":

- spaciousness
- seclusion (being alone)
- artifice (created by humans)
- antiquity (something very old)
- water features
- panoramas (views).

The perfect garden is said to include each of these, and Kenrokuen garden in Kanazawa has them all!

Gardens

Japan has many beautiful gardens, and these are often found in temples. There are said to be three great gardens in Japan. One of these is Kenrokuen in Kanazawa, which is filled with a variety of trees, ponds, waterfalls, and flowers.

Temples

Japan has many beautiful temples and shrines. The most famous of these is perhaps the Kinkaku-ji Temple in Kyoto. This is a Zen Buddhist temple, and it has many buildings. One of these is called the Golden Pavilion, which is covered in real **gold leaf**.

The Ryoan-ji Temple in Kyoto is famous for its Zen garden. This garden consists of 15 rocks arranged on white gravel within a small space. There are no trees, ponds, or flowers. Its simplicity is meant to make you use your imagination. No one knows who created this amazing garden.

This is the Zen garden at Ryoan-ji Temple. What do you see—clouds in the sky, or islands in a sea?

Clothes and fashion

The kimono is a traditional form of clothing worn by Japanese women and men. People started wearing kimonos as we know them today in the Heian period (794 CE–1185). They were made using the "straight-line-cut" method, which involves cutting pieces of material in straight lines. This meant that they could be made without thinking about any particular body shape. They were cool in summer and could be worn in layers in winter.

Kimonos do not have buttons, zips, or ties. They are held in place by an *obi*. This is a long, wide sash, which is wound around the waist and tied at the back, often in a pillow-like shape. An *obi* can be 12 feet (3.7 meters) long! They are often decorated with beautiful **embroidery** or brocade.

Geta sandals are raised on either a split or a single platform. This is to keep the kimono out of the mud! They are worn with *tabi* socks, which have split toes.

Today, Japanese people rarely wear kimonos. They save them for occasions such as weddings, funerals, tea ceremonies, or other festivals. Japanese people mainly wear Western-style clothes, and in places such as Tokyo, in particular, you will see many people with very modern clothes and hair.

Rei Kawakubo (born 1942)

Rei Kawakubo is a fashion designer. She set up the globally successful fashion company Comme des Garçons (French for "like the boys") in Tokyo in the 1970s. Kawakubo became famous for clothes that had frayed, unsewn edges and holes that look like lace. This model is wearing Kawakubo's designs at Paris Fashion Week in 2010.

Origami

Origami is a traditional Japanese pastime that is now popular all over the world. A single square of paper is folded in different ways to create shapes like animals and plants. The best-known origami shape is a crane. Origami is often taught in schools, and there are magazines and classes for adults, too. Origami can be used for gifts, wedding decorations, or simply as ornaments.

Akira Yoshizawa (1911–2005)

Akira Yoshizawa is considered to be the grandmaster of origami. He created more than 50,000 origami figures, many of which are amazingly complicated. He also set up the International Origami Center in Tokyo. He was given the Order of the Rising Sun by Emperor Hirohito in 1983, which is one of the highest honors that anyone can receive in Japan.

Bonsai

Bonsai are trees and shrubs that are grown in pots, and they are not meant to be more than 3.3 feet (1 meter) high. They are pruned (cut) and trained to grow in certain shapes so that they look like miniature versions of full-sized trees growing in a forest. Some bonsai trees live for hundreds of years and are passed down from one generation to the next.

The branches of bonsai trees have to be cut or tied onto wires to encourage them to grow a certain way. This is partly to limit their growth, but also to make them grow into beautiful shapes. Many bonsai are grown at home, but some are displayed in public gardens or in shrines.

These tiny bonsai trees are displayed outdoors.

Manga

Manga comics are usually about 150 to 350 pages long. They contain about 15 stories, are cheap to buy, and are designed to be read very fast. The same characters reappear in story after story. Japanese people of all ages read manga comics.

Manga comics present their characters in an appealing way. Even the villains continue to appear in story after story. The manga style is often quite similar to movies, using close-ups and different angles. Sometimes one expression or movement can be shown developing over several pictures.

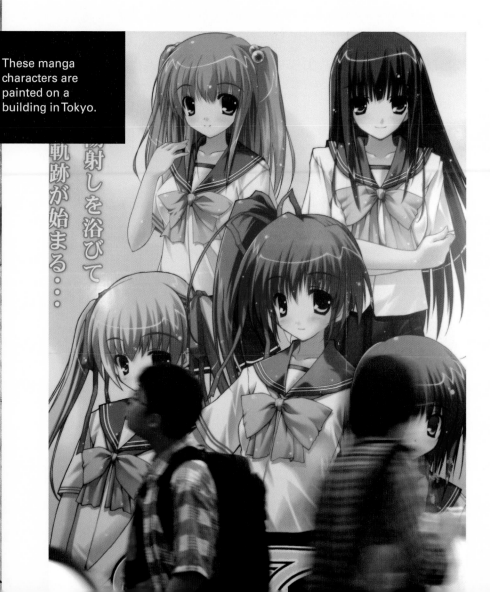

These manga characters are painted on a building in Tokyo.

Anime

Anime is a popular Japanese cartoon style. It has become very popular in Western culture, too—for example, in television series such as the *Power Rangers*. The movie *Spirited Away* won an Oscar in 2002 for Best Animated Feature. Japan is one of the largest producers of animation in the world, with Studio Ghibli, in Tokyo, leading the way.

Anime continues to be drawn by hand, although computers are now used, too. Not every single movement is animated. Sometimes characters move only their mouths when they speak. However, the animation still aims to convey lots of movement and emotion. Anime often features fantastical creatures such as Pikachu in *Pokémon*.

The two-dimensional style of anime pictures, such as this image of Astro Boy, is very similar to that used in manga comics.

Osamu Tezuka (1928–1989)

Osamu Tezuka is known as the "God of Manga." He revolutionized the Japanese cartoon and comic industries, creating hundreds of comics and dozens of movies, including *Astro Boy* (2009).

PERFORMANCE

Japanese performing arts include both ancient and modern forms, from traditional **Kabuki** and **Noh** theater and the distinctive sound of the **koto** to the massively popular karaoke!

Music and instruments

The *koto* is one of the most famous Japanese traditional instruments. It is a large wooden instrument with 13 strings, similar to a harp. It can be up to 6.5 feet (2 meters) long and 8 inches (20 centimeters) across. The *koto* is played with picks held by the fingers, similar to those sometimes used by guitarists. The instrument is rarely played now, but is sometimes heard during *hanami* cherry blossom celebrations. A smaller type of *koto* has been developed for use in classrooms.

The pitch of notes on the *koto* is adjusted by movable bridges placed under each string.

Traditional Japanese drums are known as **taiko** or *wadaiko* drums. They have been played for over 1,000 years. They can be very large, and they are often played in temples and in the theater.

A *shakuhachi* is a traditional bamboo flute, although many are now made of plastic. It only has four holes in the front and one at the back, but it can still make a wide range of notes.

Sometimes *taiko* drums can be much larger than a person!

YOUNG PEOPLE

Many children in Japan, and all over the world, have learned to play the violin by the Suzuki method. This involves listening to, copying, and repeating notes, rather than reading music. This method was created by the Japanese violinist and teacher Shinichi Suzuki.

Karaoke

Karaoke in Japanese means "empty orchestra." People sing into a microphone to a backing track of the song of their choice, following the song words that are displayed on a screen.

Karaoke began in Japan in the 1970s, and it is now popular all over the world. However, nowhere is it as widely and frequently enjoyed as in Japan! There are many karaoke stores and bars all over the country, where people can meet up to sing a wide range of hit songs and have fun.

YOUNG PEOPLE

Karaoke is so popular in Japan that there are even children's karaoke rooms that can be used for parties. Karaoke contests are often held during the *hanami* festival.

Karaoke clubs offer "boxes" of various sizes, where friends can sing and perform together.

J-pop

J-pop is modern pop music originating in Japan, and as with pop music from any other country, it has a wide range of styles and influences. In the 1990s, bands such as Pizzicato Five and Plus-Tech Squeeze Box played a mixture of jazz, pop, electropop, and computer sounds. More recently, the boy band Kanjani8 has used rap as well as Japanese folk songs in its hits.

Did you know?

Kanjani8 is a very popular Japanese boy band. In addition to singing, the band members also host television and radio programs and perform in the theater.

The name of the band is a mix of "Kansai" and "Johnny." This is because they come from the Kansai region. This is in the main island of Honshu, which includes the city of Kyoto, Japan's ancient capital. The "Johnny" in the name comes from a big Japanese music and movie company called Johnny's Entertainment, which manages the band.

Anime songs are a big part of Japanese modern popular music. These are songs sung by a *seiyu*, an actor who voices a character from an anime movie. These songs explore the feelings and ideas of the character and help the audience to understand them. Often the songs are released separately from the movie. *Seiyu* actors can become very famous in Japan, and some even have their own fan clubs.

Traditional theater

Kabuki theater is a traditional form of popular drama that involves singing and dancing. The Japanese word *ka-bu-ki* means "song-dance-skill." Costumes and makeup are used to show a character's personality and mood. Traditional *Kabuki* roles include the man of courage (*tachiyaku*), the evil man (*katakiyaku*), and the comic character (*dokegata*).

Kabuki was originally performed by women, but Japanese society began to find this improper. This meant that men took over, and soon only they were allowed to perform onstage.

Noh theater is very different. It is Japan's oldest form of musical theater. *Noh* performers are storytellers who use their appearance and movement to suggest the basic idea of a story. There is little speech, with all the focus on the movement and music. The actors often wear painted wooden masks and elaborate silk costumes.

These actors are taking part in a *Kabuki* performance. They are both male actors, but the one on the left is playing a woman.

Bunraku is a traditional form of puppet theater that uses large puppets of up to 3.3 feet (1 meter) tall. It takes a lot of skill to move the puppets, most of which require three puppeteers each. The shows are accompanied by chanting and music played on the *shamisen*, a three-stringed instrument.

Bunraku puppeteers are usually hidden from the audience's view in black cloaks and hoods.

LEISURE AND COMMUNITY

The Japanese tend to work long hours, and they used to work a regular 48-hour week. In 1993 the government changed the law to limit the working week to 40 hours, with the aim of making Japan "a great country to live in." This change meant that the Japanese had more time for leisure activities.

Sports

Baseball is the most popular team sport in Japan. It was introduced in the 1870s. Soccer is also very popular. Japan co-hosted the 2002 World Cup finals with South Korea.

Oh Sadaharu (born 1940)

Oh Sadaharu played professional baseball for the Tokyo Yomiuri from 1959 to 1980. He holds the record for the most home runs ever hit and is one of Japan's best-known sports figures.

Martial arts

Japan is famous for its martial arts, such as judo, karate, and aikido. In judo the key to beating an opponent is to take advantage of his or her strength. The main aim is to throw your opponent and defend yourself. Karate is more direct and aggressive, and it involves landing blows on your opponent's body.

Aikido is a more defensive martial art, and it emphasizes the importance of achieving calmness and control of your body. Respect toward one's opponents plays an important role in all Japanese martial arts.

Ryôko Tani (born 1975)

Ryôko Tani (right) is a famous *judoka* (judo player). She has won five Olympic medals, including two gold medals. She is very popular in Japan, where she is known as Yawara-chan, after a manga character. After Tani retired from judo in 2010, she went into politics to promote and encourage Japanese sports.

Japanese food

Traditional Japanese food is cooked very little, or not at all. It is made very carefully, and the appearance of the food is almost as important as the taste. Some examples of Japanese dishes are cherry blossom–scented rice served with a cherry blossom and salted cherry leaf, and tiny squid served in wasabi (green horseradish) sauce. Japanese food is eaten around the world.

Sushi is cooked rice, flavored with vinegar and made into balls or rolls that use a variety of vegetables, egg, and raw seafood. The balls or rolls are often stuck together with wasabi, and they are usually eaten with soy sauce. There are many sushi restaurants in Japan—and now around the world, too.

With lots of patience and practice, sushi can be made at home.

Teriyaki involves grilling beef, chicken, and fish with a highly flavored glaze of soy sauce and sake (an alcoholic drink made from fermented rice) or *mirin* (sweet rice wine).

Sashimi is fresh fish that is served raw. The fish is either cubed, cut into strips, or sliced into paper-thin slices. It is served with wasabi and soy sauce.

The Japanese eat food with chopsticks. You hold the pair of sticks in one hand and carry the food to your mouth.

Did you know?

The Japanese word for "meal" is *gohan*. This actually means "boiled rice," but rice is such an important food to the Japanese that *gohan* has come to mean all sorts of meals, even Western ones such as hamburgers.

Books and storytelling

Japan has one of the highest rates of literacy (ability to read and write) in the world. The Japanese read a great deal, from books to magazines and manga comics. Japan is one of the world's major book publishing countries.

Manga books are popular with both adults and children.

Haiku

A haiku is a short poem made up of exactly 17 syllables. These are divided into three lines of five, seven, and five syllables each. Haiku use simple text to convey thoughts and emotions, particularly about the seasons. Here is an example of a haiku that was originally written in English:

Heavy summer rain:
The petals of the roses
Bow down with water.

Games

Shogi is the Japanese form of chess. The object of the game is to checkmate, or trap, the opposing king. The rules are similar to chess, but with one major difference: a player can capture an opponent's piece and put it into play as his or her own piece.

Go originated in China over 4,000 years ago, and it has been played in Japan for centuries. Two players take turns placing black or white pieces on a board. The board is covered with a grid, and the player who conquers the most territory wins. As with chess, learning *go* strategy can take a lifetime.

YOUNG PEOPLE

Japanese children love playing *shogi* and *go*. Children as young as 11 years old may even start training as professional players.

Music players and phones

Much of the technology we use every day started in Japan. The country is one of the world leaders in developing new technology.

The portable Sony personal stereo, or "Walkman," was launched in Japan in 1979, followed by the first compact disc player in 1982. Both of these players had a huge effect on how music was listened to and shared with others. In 1979 the first commercial cell phone network was started in Tokyo. Now, the Japanese use cell phones more than landline phones.

Did you know?

You can find vending machines everywhere in Japan. They sell everything from newspapers and clothes to eggs and flowers!

Cell phones are now a big part of everyday life for the Japanese—and for the rest of the world.

Electronic games

As with music players and phones, many electronic games and consoles were developed in Japan. In 1994 Sony launched the PlayStation, which allowed players to play together using handheld controllers. In 2006 Nintendo produced the first Wii consoles. With a Wii control, players can move characters or perform a variety of activities— such as playing golf, playing the guitar, or dancing—by performing actions and movements with a wireless remote control.

Shigeru Miyamoto (born 1952)

Shigeru Miyamoto is a video game designer and producer who created some of the most famous computer characters and games ever, including Donkey Kong and Mario.

Wii has made playing computer games a more social activity.

These Japanese innovations led the way in helping to make computer games more social and interactive—and now the Japanese, along with the rest of the world, play online, too.

JAPANESE CULTURE IN THE 21ST CENTURY

Japanese culture is full of contrasts. The Japanese are aware of their traditions, such as festivals, *Noh* theater, and tea ceremonies. However, their culture is also constantly developing with new music, fashion, and technologies.

Tradition is still a big part of life in Japan.

Japanese designs are often decorative, such as the designs on *Kabuki* costumes. However, simplicity is also prized. The Zen gardens of Ryoan-ji are artificial, but they feel natural and harmonious. Tea ceremonies emphasize the importance of paying attention to the smallest details. At the same time, they are about escaping the everyday world and offering people a chance to think about themselves and others.

The Japanese tell stories about traditional heroes in manga comics and anime movies, which are appealing to today's audiences. Japanese people are rooted in Eastern traditions, but they are also heavily influenced by Western culture.

The Japanese people have created a vibrant culture with lots of different influences. It will be fascinating to see what the future holds.

There is a love of nature in Japanese culture, as the *hanami* cherry blossom celebrations show. However, many Japanese people live in modern cities full of the latest technology. They also know how to enjoy themselves at a karaoke party!

There is one thing you can say for sure about Japanese culture: it is full of surprises, and more of them are yet to come.

TIMELINE

300 BCE–300 CE (Yayoi period) The first *taiko* drums are
brought to Japan

CE

500	*Go* is introduced to Japan
710–784	(Nara period) *Hanami* (cherry blossom celebrations) begin; the first *kotos* are made
794–1185	(Heian period) The first kimonos are made
1309	First record of bonsai trees being grown is made
1338–1573	(Muromachi period) First *Noh* theater is performed
1397	Temple of the Golden Pavilion is built in Kyoto
about 1500	The Ryoan-ji Temple and garden are built
1603	The first *Kabuki* theater begins
1800s	The first modern manga comic strips appear
1870s	Baseball is introduced to Japan
1970s	Karaoke begins in Japan
1979	The first commercial cell phone network is set up in Japan
1982	The first compact disc player is made in Japan
1985	Studio Ghibli (a maker of anime movies) is founded
1994	Sony launches the Playstation
2002	Japan hosts the World Cup with South Korea
2006	Nintendo launches the Wii

CULTURAL MAP

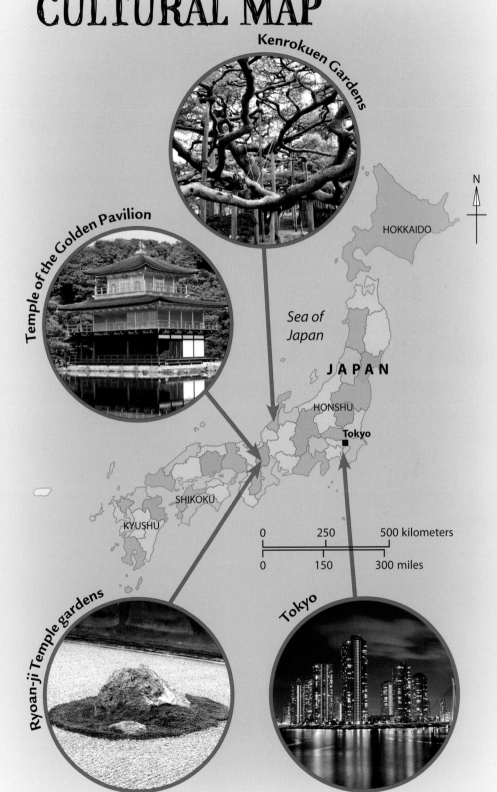

Kenrokuen Gardens

Temple of the Golden Pavilion

HOKKAIDO

Sea of Japan

JAPAN

HONSHU

Tokyo

SHIKOKU

KYUSHU

Ryoan-ji Temple gardens

Tokyo

N

| 0 | 250 | 500 kilometers |

| 0 | 150 | 300 miles |

GLOSSARY

anime popular cartoon style used in television series and movies

bonsai miniature tree or shrub that has been artificially grown

Buddhist person who follows the religion of Buddhism, which began in India in the 5th century BCE

bunraku traditional puppet theater

calligraphy decorative handwriting

ceremony acts and behavior on an important occasion

culture customs, social organization, and achievements of a particular nation, people, or group

embroidery art of sewing designs on clothes

gold leaf extremely thin sheets of gold

haiku short poem made up of exactly 17 syllables

hanami traditional custom of celebrating and enjoying the cherry blossom season

hierarchy system in which people or things are ordered according to their importance

Kabuki traditional drama, including singing and dancing

kimono traditional form of clothing with long sleeves and no buttons or ties

koto large wooden instrument with 13 strings

manga comic with serialized characters and a distinctive style

meditation clearing the mind and controlling the breathing

Noh Japan's oldest form of musical theater, with a focus on movement and music

nuclear family father, mother, and children

origami folding a single square of paper to create shapes

seiyu actor who voices a character from an anime movie

shrine building or small structure that is devoted to a religion

spiritual concerned with one's inner being or soul, as opposed to physical and material things

sushi cooked rice, flavored with vinegar and vegetables, eggs, and raw seafood

syllable smallest unit of sound into which a word can be broken down. For example, there are three syllables in the word "Ja-pa-nese."

taiko traditional Japanese drums

tatami woven grass mat

temple building or place of worship of a religion

zabuton cushion used on *tatami* matting

FIND OUT MORE

Books

Catel, Patrick. *Japan* (Countries Around the World).
Chicago: Heinemann Library, 2012.

Hardyman, Robyn. *Japan* (Celebrate!). New York: Chelsea
Clubhouse, 2009.

Phillips, Charles. *Japan* (Countries of the World). Washington,
D.C.: National Geographic Society, 2009.

Pipe, Jim. *Japan* (Countries in Our World). Mankato, Minn.:
Smart Apple Media, 2012.

Websites

https://www.cia.gov/library/publications/the-world-fact-
book/geos/ja.html
The World Factbook has a profile of Japan, with information
on its geography, people, and more.

kids.asiasociety.org/explore/childrens-day-japan-kodomo-
no-hi
Read all about Children's Day in Japan, and learn how to
make your own *koinobori* kite.

kids.nationalgeographic.com/kids/places/find/japan/
Find photos, videos, maps, and activities about Japan.

web-japan.org/kidsweb
Learn more about Japanese life, including topics like manga.

DVDs

My Neighbor Totoro (1988, reissued 2006)
Spirited Away (2001)

Places to visit

The Freer Gallery of Art and the Arthur M. Sackler Gallery, Washington, D.C.

www.asia.si.edu

The Freer and Sackler Galleries contain over 11,000 examples of Japanese art, ranging from calligraphy to baskets to paintings.

The Japanese American National Museum, Los Angeles, California

www.janm.org

The Japanese American National Museum has over 60,000 artifacts, documents, and photographs about the experience and artwork of Japanese Americans.

Metropolitan Museum of Art, New York City

www.metmuseum.org

The Metropolitan Museum of Art has many galleries dedicated to Japanese art.

Portland Japanese Garden, Portland, Oregon

japanesegarden.com

The Portland Japanese Garden is a traditional Japanese garden. It is considered one of the world's finest Japanese gardens outside of Japan.

More topics to research

What topic did you like reading about most in this book? Did you find out anything that you thought was particularly interesting? Choose a topic that you liked, such as food, buildings, or religion, and try to find out more about it. You could visit one of the places mentioned above, take a look at one of the websites listed here, or visit your local library to do some research. You could also try writing your own haiku, enjoying an anime movie, or trying out some sushi!

INDEX